THE PALETTE OF INDIA

AN EXPLORATION OF THE ARTISTIC TRADITION AND CULTURAL HERITAGE OF INDIA

DR. JAGADEESH PILLAI

|| "Dedicated to all who seek to understand and appreciate Indian culture and tradition." ||

ॐ

Contents

Contents

PRAYER

**"Om Poornamadah Poornamidam Poornat
Poornamudachyate,Poornasya Poornamaadaya
Poornamevavashishyate,Om Shantih, Shantih, Shantih"**

*The literal interpretation of this mantra is: That which is
Absolute, This which is Absolute, Absolute arises from Absolute,
If Absolute is removed from Absolute, Absolute remains
OM Peace, Peace, Peace.*

About The Author

Dr. Jagadeesh Pillai is a renowned Guinness World Record holder, writer, and researcher hailing from Varanasi, also known as the abode of Lord Shiva. With a Ph.D. in Vedic Science and a range of creative ideas and achievements, he is a true polymath. He is the author of more than 100 books including Research Publications. Although his roots can be traced back to Kerala, the people of Varanasi hold him in high regard and affectionately consider him one of their own.

Dr. Pillai has achieved four Guinness World Records in the following subjects:

"Script to Screen" - In this record, Dr. Pillai produced and directed an animation film within the shortest time possible, breaking the previous record set by Canadians. He has also received numerous national and international awards and recognitions for this achievement.

Longest Line of Postcards - For this record, Dr. Pillai created a line of 16,300 postcards on the occasion of the 163rd anniversary of Indian Postal Day. The event also included a questionnaire about the Indian flag.

Largest Poster Awareness Campaign - Dr. Pillai designed an awareness campaign on the subject of "Beti Bachao - Beti Padhao" (Save the Girl Child - Educate the Girl Child) to achieve this record.

Largest Envelope - In tribute to the Indian Prime Minister's

"Make in India" initiative, Dr. Pillai created a 4000 square meter envelope using waste paper to achieve this record.

Attempted - **70000 Candles on a 210 kg Cake** - To celebrate the 70th Indian Independence Day, Dr. Pillai attempted to light 70,000 candles on a 210 kg cake, which was recorded in World Records India.

Attempted - **Documentary on Dhamek Stupa of Sarnath in 17 Languages** - Dr. Pillai attempted to create a documentary on the Dhamek Stupa of Sarnath, dubbing it in 17 different languages. The result of this attempt is currently awaiting confirmation from the Guinness World Records.

Dr. Pillai is skilled in teaching the Bhagavad Gita, a Hindu scripture, and is popular among young people. He has helped many young people improve their lives through his motivational teachings.

In addition to teaching, he has composed and sung numerous Sanskrit Bhajans and patriotic songs.

He has also written and directed several short films and documentaries for awareness campaigns, and has volunteered with the police in both UP and Kerala to spread awareness about various issues through videos and photography.

Incredibly, he has produced and directed over 100 documentaries about the city of Varanasi, all on his own.

He has also helped and guided more than 25 boys and girls to achieve world records through creative and innovative methods. He is a multifaceted person who uses his intellect and the blessings given to him by God to excel in various areas. He is both a teacher and a student, always learning and teaching, and is able to master any subject he comes across.

He is a selfless social activist and motivational speaker who has overcome struggles and failures to become a successful and enthusiastic individual with a rich life experience.

In addition to his work with the Bhagavad Gita, he is also an efficient Tarot card reader, Astro-Vastu consultant, and a talented singer and composer. He has sung the entire Ram Charita Manas and Bhagavad Gita in his own compositions, and has sung the phrase "Lokah Samastha Sukhino Bhavantu" in 50 different languages. He is currently working on a detailed and scientific study of Vedas, Upanishads, Puranas, and the Bhagavad Gita. He has also composed and sung the Hanuman Chalisa and Gayatri Mantra in 108 and 1008 different compositions, respectively.

Awards - Four Times Guinness World Records, Winner of Mahatma Gandhi Vishwa Shanti Puraskar, Mahatma Gandhi Global Peace Ambassador, Kashi Ratna Award, Dr. APJ Abdul Kalam Motivational Person of the Year 2017, Mother Teresa Award, Indira Gandhi Priyadarshini Award, Bharat Vikas Ratna Award, Udyog Ratna Award, Vigyan Prasar Award, Poorvanchal Ratn Samman.

Preface

The Indian subcontinent has a rich and diverse history of art and painting, dating back to ancient times. From the intricate carvings of the Harappan civilization to the vibrant frescoes of the Ajanta caves, Indian art has always been a reflection of the country's culture, history, and way of life.

The book, "The Palette of India: An Exploration of the Artistic Tradition and Cultural Heritage of India," aims to provide readers with a comprehensive understanding of the Indian art and painting industry and its various components. The book explores the history and culture of Indian art and painting, and covers a wide range of topics, including ancient Indian art, medieval Indian art, Mughal art, Rajput art, and modern Indian art.

The book draws on research from a variety of sources, including interviews with artists, art historians, and curators, archival materials, and cultural analysis. I have also conducted extensive field research in India, including visiting art galleries, museums, and historical sites, and interviewing artists and artisans.

I am deeply passionate about the beauty of Indian art and painting, and I hope that this book will help to spread the appreciation of this wonderful form of expression. I believe that the Indian artistic tradition has a great deal to offer to the world and I am excited to share its cultural and historical significance with my readers.

This book is intended for a wide audience, including art enthusiasts, students, researchers, and anyone interested in the history and culture of Indian art and painting. It is my hope that this book will serve as a valuable resource for those interested in learning more about the Indian artistic tradition and its role in shaping the country's culture and history.

It is important to note that this book is intended for informational and educational purposes only, and should not be used as a substitute for professional art historical analysis or as a complete guide to Indian art and painting. The contents of this book are based on the author's research and opinions, and should not be taken as fact.

I

Introduction: Understanding Indian Art and Painting

Indian art and painting is an ancient and influential tradition that is rooted in the cultural and religious beliefs of the culture and country. From the early cave paintings of the Indus Valley civilization to the elaborate works of the Moguls and Hindu dynasties, Indian art and painting have been deeply shaped by India's unique and varied religious, cultural and political history. India's rich past has given rise to a sophisticated and vibrant body of art and painting that continues to have a significant impact on the world today.

In order to understand Indian art and painting, it is important to look at its historical context. Indian art and painting have been greatly influenced by a variety of religions, such as Buddhism, Hinduism, Jainism, and Islam. These religions have provided Indian art and painting with unique themes and motifs that have made their way into the imagery used in Indian art and painting. This is especially true of Hinduism, which has had the greatest influence on Indian art and painting. With its complex pantheon of gods and goddesses, Hinduism has given Indian art and painting an instantly recognizable and single cultural look. Furthermore, each Hindu deity has a representation in painting or sculpture, which makes Indian art and painting easily recognizable and familiar.

In addition to its religious influence, Indian art and painting have been greatly shaped by its geographic location. Located at the crossroads of major trade routes and cultural exchange, Indian art and painting have been greatly enriched by influences from the Middle East, Central Asia, and even Africa. This led to the development of a myriad of artistic styles and techniques, which have come to define Indian art and painting. This includes a variety of miniature painting techniques, woodblock printing techniques, and intricate stone and bronze carving techniques. As a result of these foreign influences, Indian art and painting became a vibrant mix of styles that blended elements from East and West, Hindu and Muslim, and traditional and modern.

Finally, it is also important to understand that Indian art and painting have become an important cultural export. Indian art and painting are highly treasured and appreciated around the world, and can be found in some of the world's most exclusive galleries and museums. India's art and painting have become a symbol of its rich culture and history, and its influence is still present in modern-day art and design. Indian art and painting are a reflection of the vibrant, multifaceted culture of India, and is an invaluable part of the country's cultural identity.

Indian art and painting is a unique and fascinating art form that is deeply rooted in the religious, cultural, and political history of India. It has been greatly influenced by India's various religions, as well as by its geographic location and foreign influences. Furthermore, Indian art and painting are highly appreciated around the world and have become an important cultural export from India.

"The conception of Indian art and painting must be viewed and appreciated through symbolism, which is the language of the soul."
– Ananda K Coomaraswamy

II

Art & Painting of India- Mauryan & Gupta Period

Classical art & painting of India during the Mauryan and Gupta Periods represent some of the most beautiful & impressive art of ancient India. These artworks reflect the high level of creativity of the artists & the people of that period.

In the Mauryan period, art primarily focused on depictions of animals & deities. Various murals, sculptures, & pottery of this period can be found in various places of India. The lion & bull sculptures at the Sanchi Stupa are among the most remarkable works of Mauryan art. These were created in order to honour the Sun god, Surya. Other artworks of this period include the famous Ashoka Pillar at Sarnath, which is a testimony to the largely tolerant Buddhist rulers of the Maurya Empire.

The Gupta Period is known as the 'golden age' of Indian art. During this time, Indian art evolved in various styles & techniques. The most popular of these styles was naturalism & it was characteristic of paintings of this period. Examples of the naturalistic style can be seen in various paintings & sculptures, including the Sarnath Sculptures and the Ajanta Caves murals. These works gave rise to various Indian artistic traditions such as darbar paintings, miniature paintings, bharatabirang paintings, & mughal paintings.

The Gupta period also saw great advancements in mural painting. This can be seen in various pieces of art such as the Ajantha murals & the Ajanta sculptures. These pieces of art feature highly polished detail & elegant lines. They depict scenes from the Mahabharata, the Ramayana, & various other religious stories from Hindu mythology.

In the medieval period, the Indian art of painting was further developed by different rulers. This period saw the emergence of miniature paintings, which combined traditional Indian painting styles & foreign trends. During this period, many different styles of painting emerged, such as Rajasthani, Deccani, & Mughal. These styles displayed precise details & a unique sense of perspective, offering a unique insight into the art of the past.

The classical art & painting of India during the Mauryan & Gupta periods were a reflection of the advanced artistic culture of ancient India. The artworks of this period are still admired today & offer an insight into the lifestyle & culture of the period. These artworks stand as a testament to the skill & ingenuity of the Indian people during that time.

"Indian art is the expression of India's spiritual identity,
rooted in her ancient spiritual lessons that have been
handed down to us, generation after generation."
– Satyajit Ray

III

The Post-Gupta Period Art & Painting: Regional styles & influences

The Post-Gupta Period in India heralded a period of great artistic and cultural progress and traditions. From the 5th century AD to the 12th century AD, this period marked the emergence of numerous different regional styles of Indian art and painting. It also saw the introduction of new for the region -styles of painting, such as Qadam-e-Shirazi. These regional styles and influences that emerged in this period were highly influential for centuries thereafter.

In the North, especially in modern-day Uttar Pradesh,

Bihar, and Bengal, the Post-Gupta style of art and painting was particularly strong. This was due in part to the establishment of major centers of learning such as those at Nalanda and Vikramashila. The art and painting in this region blended the Persian influence of the Post-Gupta period with local styles. This produced a unique style of painting, termed the "Gulali" style. This style featured intricate designs and vivid colors, and was often used to illustrate religious stories and epics.

To the South, the legacy of the Cholas, Pandyas, and Pallavas in the region played a major role in determining the regional styles of art and painting. This Southern region produced its own distinctive painting style, which was heavily influenced by Indian sculptures. This style featured depictions of religious figures as well as nature and often incorporated intricate jewelry, textiles, and decorative patterns. The Asokan Pillars at Mahabalipuram are a fine example of regional painting style from this period.

Finally, in the West, the Rashtrakuta, Pratihara, and Chalukya dynasties exerted great influence upon the art and painting of the period. This area was especially influenced by the migration of Deccan artists and their subsequent blending of Persian and Indian styles. The accompanying painting traditions tended towards a colorful and distinctive Artwork, often in the form of illuminated manuscripts. One of the best-known examples of such Illuminations is found in the Jain Manuscripts of the Ellora Khoh Cave paintings.

The Post-Gupta period produced an impressive array of regional styles and influences upon Indian art and painting. Such styles and influences had a far-reaching and long-lasting impact, and helped to develop and diversify the Indian artistic heritage.

"Indian painting is characterized by its use of bold
colors, intricate details and its boldness."
– Nandalal Bose

ॐ

IV

The Cave Paintings and Rock-cut Temples of India

India, a diverse country full of mystifying culture and ancient relics often draws the attention of numerous historians, archaeologists, and travelers alike who can't help but be entranced by its enigmatic past. One particularly outstanding piece of this ancient culture are the rock-cut temples and cave paintings that can be found throughout India. Over the centuries, these remnants of ancient India have caught the eyes of countless people, many of which appreciate the ethereal aspects and timeless beauty of the artwork.

The cave paintings found in India are some of the oldest and most renowned in the world. These paintings, which can most commonly be found in the Vadnagar region of Gujarat, are considered to be part of a primitive form of art dating hundreds of thousands of years back. These paintings demonstrate agricultural scenes, different animals, and portraits of humanoids and are believed to be depictions of ancient religious activity. Not only do these paintings provide snapshots of old rituals, but they also demonstrate the extent to which ancient Indians indulged in aesthetic adornment in the distant past.

The rock-cut temples of India are another impressive piece of history that continues to captivate many travelers. These temples, which date back to the ancient days of the second century, are located in many places such as Bidar, Aurangabad, and Badami in the state of Karnataka. These polytheistic temples are an exemplary display of the rich Hindu and Buddhist tradition that prevailed in India for centuries. Carved into various stone monoliths, these magnificent temples form intricate scenes of deities, intricate sculptures, and grand mandapas. As if it weren't already astounding enough, these monolithic temples also contain underground channels that have a surprise located at their end, namely stunning water fountains.

Both of these elements of ancient India have proved to be remarkable records of history, art, and culture. The cave paintings have managed to capture and encapsulate religious rituals, while the rock-cut temples hold together centuries worth of ethnic and religious history. These elements of India remain interactive pieces of our past in the present day and captivate the audience with their evocative beauty. Together, they prove to be an unmissable part of India's culture and are sure to dazzle generations of travelers for years to come.

ॐ

"Indian painting is the expression of something metaphysical."
– Rabindranath Tagore

V

The Mural Paintings of South India

The Mural Paintings of South India are considered to be some of the most beautiful and fascinating works of art in the region. Spanning over four thousand years, these paintings represent an important part of the region's cultural heritage and have been admired by people for their intricate designs, vibrant colors, and detailed narratives.

The Mural Paintings of South India originated from ancient temples, caves, and tombs located on the Western Ghat Mountains, dating back to the 8th century B.C. and continuing until the 18th century. These works of art range from representing scenes from the Ramayana, Mahabharata, and several Bhakti literature and some also depicted scenes from everyday life. The paintings are also related to different Hindu gods and goddesses like Vishnu,

Shiva, Durga, and also Buddhist figures.

The Mural Paintings of South India were mainly produced using watercolors and mineral paints. The durability of these paintings was ensured by applying several coats of gum arabic and then a coat of lime. The bright pigments of red, yellow, green, and blue help the paintings to remain visible even after hundreds of years.

The art of Mural Painting in South India is highly stylized and intricate. Many of the works feature gods in traditional poses, but with a South Indian twist, which makes them distinct and attractive. The use of multiple colors, intricate geometric figures, and symbolical symbols are what gives these paintings their characteristic beauty. Every painting is an intrinsic part of the region's history. They represent significant moments and stories, making them an important part of the cultural life of the region.

Today, the Mural Paintings of South India are seen as a unique part of Indian art and heritage. They are an important reminder of the region's remoteness and past. Although many of them have been damaged and ruined due to natural disasters and weathering, it is still possible to find exquisite works of art highlighting the ancient, cultural heritage of the region.

"Indian painting is a celebration of life and its many
mysteries."
– Nandalal Bose

VI

The Miniature Paintings of North India

The miniature paintings of North India are known for their exquisite creations and captivating beauty. These paintings possess a unique and timeless charm which is indicative of the rich cultural heritage of India.

Miniature paintings originated as small-scale religious art, depicting Hindu gods and goddesses, as well as scenes from Hindu religious texts. From this time, the tradition of miniature painting was passed down through generations, adapting and evolving over the years in order to create unique styles and techniques.

The tradition of miniature painting was particularly popular in the Princely States of Rajasthan, Gujarat and Punjab. There, it was popularised by the Mughal emperors who brought the art form to their court. These Mughal rulers employed the services of talented painters to create miniature paintings which they could adorn their palaces with, capturing the grandeur and majesty of the Mughal dynasty.

The most distinctive feature of North Indian miniature painting is its high degree of detail. The painting can take up to several days to complete, and each brush stroke is carefully and meticulously detailed. Every single element of the painting is designed to capture the spirit and emotion of the subject. The colour palette that is used is also highly saturated, using bright and vivid colours which create a captivating and beautiful effect.

North Indian miniature painting is particularly popular for its depiction of court scenes. These paintings portray kings and queens, courtiers, warriors and court musicians, all of whom appear as part of a larger scene. While the main theme is always the same, unique and personalised details, such as costumes and jewelry, are added in order to create a more personalised and authentic feel.

North Indian miniature painting is known for its exquisite details and captivating beauty. From its beginnings as religious art, miniature painting has evolved and adapted over the years in order to create stunning works of art that capture the grandeur and majesty of the Princely States of Rajasthan, Gujarat and Punjab. Whether it be court scenes, or religious depictions, North Indian miniature painting has enchanted viewers for centuries, and will likely continue to do so for many years to come.

౫౨

DR. JAGADEESH PILLAI

"The origins of Indian painting are expressions of spiritual ideas and mysteries, rather than simply aesthetic tradition."
– Ananda K Coomaraswamy

VII
The Folk and Tribal Art of India

India is a country rich in cultural diversity, and its people take great pride in their traditional and folk art forms. For centuries, folk and tribal art has been passed down from generations in order to keep their identity alive.

The folk and tribal art of India can be divided into two main forms – visual arts and performing arts. The wide variety of visual arts includes paintings, carvings, jewellery-making, metal work, pottery, and stone sculptures. These techniques are often used to create murals and symbols unique to a certain community that signify important events and beliefs.

Performing arts are seen as one of the most important aspects of Indian culture and identity. Traditional dance forms, such as Bharat Natyam, Manipuri, and Odissi, are often used to express stories and messages to the audience.

Music is another popular form of expression in India, with a wide variety of instruments being used to create works that reflect local cultures and beliefs.

Folk and tribal art forms are deeply rooted in the spiritual and religious beliefs of locals, making every piece of art filled with history and tradition. For example, the Madhubani paintings of Bihar usually carry messages and initials related to Hindu gods and goddesses. Similarly, the Navratri Festival in Gujarat is celebrated with colourful dance performances and traditional musical instruments.

Folk and tribal art of India are also used for everyday items, such as clothing, household decorations, ornaments, and handicrafts. India has numerous rural artisans and craftsmen who use traditional techniques to create handmade items, ensuring the continuity of these art forms.

The folk and tribal art of India is filled with cultural values, history, and beliefs. These art forms are a celebration of India's rich diversity and unique identity. They also form a crucial part of our cultural identity and help keep the traditions of our past alive.

"Indian painting should show both the style and the relationship between the earth and the heavens."
– Raja Ravi Verma

VIII
The Rajput Paintings and Rajasthani Art

Rajasthani art and Rajput paintings depict the cultural diversity and artistic brilliance from the majestic land of Rajasthan. Rajasthani art and Rajput paintings were largely patronized by the royal families of Raja Mansingh and Raja Sawai Jai Singh of Amber and Jaipur respectively, who made great contributions in developing the various art forms of Rajasthan. They depict the history, folk tales, culture, and lifestyle of the people from the region.

The Rajput paintings mainly depict just two themes: battles between heroic forces and religious subjects like divine worship. The most popular painting styles used in Rajput painting are Mughal style and Rajput style. The Mughal style was heavily influenced by Central Asian and Persian art, while the Rajput paintings depicted heroic and religious stories through bold lines and vibrant colors. The painting often depict famous historical events such as battles. In the Rajput painting style, the figures are portrayed with disproportionately long arms and large eyes and striking costumes.

Rajasthani art is mainly constituted of the small miniature paintings of the Rajput paintings style. These miniature paintings are most often painted on canvas, which is then used to create exquisite designs on walls, doors, and other important locations. The paintings often feature unique perspectives, delicate details and complex patterns. The paintings depict a fusion of Indian folk art, Mughal and Persian patterns.

Rajasthani art also includes beautiful works of modern art such as tapestries and exquisite silk paintings. The tapestries are created with finely threaded beads, which create brilliant and vibrant designs. Similarly, the silk paintings use different intricate styles and vibrant colors to depict a range of traditional and modern scenes.

Both Rajasthani art and Rajput paintings form a vital part of Indian culture and history, by reflecting both the ancient and modern civilization of Rajasthan through their unique French and Central Asian heritage. Rajasthani art and Rajput paintings are renowned for their beautiful illustrations, vivid colours and captivating themes. These styles of art are actively practiced even today and are the source of inspiration for artists from all over the world.

"The power of Indian art and painting lies in its ability to
communicate timeless truths in unique ways."
– Abanindranath Tagore

৺

IX

The Mughal Painting & its influence on Indian Art

The Mughal painting is a type of Indian miniature painting which flourished during the Mughal Empire from the 16th to the 19th centuries. These Mughal paintings are highly detailed works of art which depict the dynastic rulers and royal events of the Mughal court. The Mughal painting style had a huge influence on Indian art, leading to the establishment of several other art forms in the country.

Mughal painting emerged during the Mughal Empire which was founded by Babur in 1525 AD. As the Mughal rulers were great patrons of art, Mughal painting flourished during their reign. These paintings usually featured rulers, military figures, religious figures, court scenes, and scenes from everyday life in the Mughal court. The paintings were often accompanied by written text and they provided an accurate historical account of the events depicted.

Mughal painting was influenced by several other styles, such as Persian painting and miniature painting. The Mughal painters used an alphabetical script, vibrant colours and intricate details to create their works of art. These paintings were highly realistic and had naturalistic facial features, feathers, and even jewellery. They were also characterised by the use of vibrant colours, such as blues, reds, greens, and yellows.

Mughal paintings had a great influence on Indian art. It led to the establishment of several art forms, such as Pahari painting, Kangra painting, and Rajput painting. It also had an influence on landscape painting, where nature and people are depicted in great detail. Furthermore, the Mughal painting style is also evident in Indian miniature painting, where similar techniques and features are used.

The Mughal painting is an important type of Indian miniature painting which flourished during the Mughal Empire from the 16th to the 19th centuries. Mughal paintings are highly detailed works of art, characterised by their use of an alphabetical script, vibrant colours and intricate details, and naturalistic facial features. Furthermore, these paintings had a great influence on Indian art, leading to the establishment of several other styles of art throughout the country.

"The purpose of Indian art and painting is to create an atmosphere of tranquility, serenity and harmony with the universe."
– Jamini Roy

X

The conservation and preservation of Indian Art

The conservation and preservation of Indian art is essential to preserving the country's cultural heritage. India is home to a vast array of art forms, ranging from ancient temple and palace architecture to modern painting and sculpture. These pieces of art, whether ancient or modern, are incredibly valuable to the culture and must be carefully preserved for future generations.

The conservation and preservation of Indian art is a complex and multi-faceted process. It involves preserving the physical structure of the artwork, as well as its aesthetic value and traditional meaning. Additionally, it is important to ensure that the artwork is protected from environmental factors, such as light, humidity, and air pollution. Furthermore, it is necessary to conserve the artwork from theft and vandalism.

The first step in the preservation of Indian art is the identification and cataloging of the artwork, as well as its condition and significance. This is followed by the development of a conservation plan, which includes the steps that must be taken to ensure the artwork's preservation. These steps include the selection of appropriate materials and techniques for conservation, the use of protective enclosures, and the proper storage and display of the artwork.

In addition to conserving and preserving the artwork itself, it is also important to preserve the artist's original intent. This includes the recognition and protection of the artist's rights and the preservation of the artwork's original meaning. This can be done through the protection of the artwork's physical integrity, as well as the promotion of its cultural value.

Overall, the conservation and preservation of Indian art is essential to preserving the country's cultural heritage. With the proper steps and resources, it is possible to ensure that the artwork is preserved for future generations. This will help to ensure that India's art remains an integral part of its cultural identity.

"Indian painting provides a great opportunity to explore
nature, beauty and the eternal truth of existence." –
Rabindranath Tagore

৪৩

XI

The British Colonial influence on Indian Art

Indian art has been shaped by a complex and ever-evolving range of influences, both internal as well as external. While many of the core traditions of Indian art are ancient, the British colonial period has had a lasting and indelible effect on the development of contemporary Indian art.

The British presence in India began with the introduction of trading outposts, and the acquisition of territories in the late 17th century. This period saw the emergence of distinct styles of painting and sculpture, drawing on both classical Indian and Western traditions. As time went on, the British presence in India came to expand its reach and influence, to the point where they completely subsumed the area, imposing their ideological, political and aesthetic perspectives on the region.

This extended period of contact with British artistic sensibilities had a great bearing on a range of art forms including painting, sculpture and architecture. At first, Indian painters responded by adapting their styles to appeal to Western sensibilities, introducing more realistic and naturalist themes with a greater focus on accurate representation of the subject. However, it was with the arrival of the British Raj during the 19th century that one of the most significant changes in Indian art took place.

The introduction of paper, pencils and watercolour paints quickly took hold, and European romantic and naturalist styles became in vogue. Photographic devices allowed for accurate and detailed reproductions of scenes from everyday life, as well as iconic architectural monuments. In the later part of the century, a number of Indian painters traveled to Europe for further education, and allowed the western tradition of 'plein-air' painting of outdoor scenes to gain greater traction upon their return.

Concurrent with the evolution of painting, sculpture also saw great changes under British influence. Hindus who had long relied upon sculpture to tell stories began to adopt the European tradition of linear, academic realism - a style which, to this day, dominates much of contemporary Indian sculpture.

The British colonial period thus shaped much of the major artistic movements in India during the 20th century. While this period was marked by the fusion of two distinct artistic traditions, it remains a point of tension for contemporary artists, who are constantly grappling with the legacy of the past, and the challenge of finding new ways to reconcile traditional Indian art and design with that of the present day. Nonetheless, the influence of the British colonial period remains unmistakable and is an important part of what makes Indian art so varied and dynamic.

"Indian painting shows a continuous evolution in technique throughout the centuries." – Raja Ravi Verma

೮

XII

The emergence of Modern Indian Art

The emergence of Modern Indian Art can be traced back to the early 19th century when the artistic techniques of European and western techniques were introduced to India. This transformation of traditional Indian art was heavily impacted by Begum Samru, an artist and ruler of Sirmur. She invited French artists to her court who taught local artists oil painting and increased the use of perspective, shade, and colors in their work. This blending of styles, where traditional Indian art combined with western techniques, marked the emergence of Modern Indian Art in the world.

Since then, numerous artists have come and gone who have shaped and evolved Modern Indian Art. One such name is Raja Ravi Varma, who is recognized as the father of Modern Indian Art with his unique use of colors and incorporation of Sanskrit epics into his work. He is credited with popularizing the Kalighat painting style in the 19th century, which was further adopted by younger generations of artist.

The first major experiment in modern art took place in the art school of Bombay in 1919. The school initiated a series of reforms, which aimed to free the Indian artists from the presence of European aesthetics. Inspired by his colleagues, Rabindranath Tagore opened the first Indian university devoted entirely to the arts and humanities, named Kala Bhavana. This provided a platform to the upcoming Indian artists to explore new ideas and experiment with the different forms of art.

The post-independence period witnessed an increase in the desire of Indian artists to express themselves through a combination of Indian and western styles. This desire culminated in an art movement known as the Indian Progressive Artists' Group in 1947. The group was led by veteran artist F. N. Souza and whose members included, K. H. Ara, M. F. Husain, and S. H. Raza among many others. The group aspired to reinterpret traditional Indian art through a contemporary Western lens and was widely accepted by the Indian public.

In the current times, Modern Indian Art is widely appreciated within the country as well as abroad. Indian artists have experimented with a range of mediums, from printmaking to sculpture to painting. They have combined popular style elements from western and traditional Indian styles, with vivid colors and abstract shapes to create unique pieces of art.

Furthermore, international exhibitions and art festivals have further propelled the debate around Modern Indian Art. It has slowly been accepted as a valid and meaningful form of art, compared to its traditional counterpart. With its newfound recognition, Modern Indian Art has begun to make an impact in the Indian art scene, with more artists stepping up to create beautiful and unique works that combine the best of both eastern and western art cultures.

"The creativity of Indian painting stems from its refusal
to adhere to any one style or form."
– Jamini Roy

৩

XIII

Indian Art in the Digital Age

Indian art is one of the oldest and most widely recognized and appreciated forms of art in the world. It has been used to adorn numerous temples, homes and public spaces around the globe. In recent times however, Indian art has experienced many changes and transformations as a result of the digital age.

The digital age has enabled Indian artists to express their art in more accessible, creative and interactive ways. Technology has enabled them to explore and experiment with new ways of creating, which have lead to the emergence of new mediums and techniques. For example, many Indian artists have taken advantage of digital platforms such as Adobe Photoshop and CorelDraw, to create digitally enhanced art works. These digital tools allow for a greater range of both playful and serious techniques, enabling them to create artworks with greater complexity and detail than ever before. Not only have these tools changed the way Indian artworks are created, but they have also allowed for the easier sharing and displaying of them across a multitude of digital platforms.

In addition, the internet has had a major impact on the way Indian art is shared and consumed. The widespread use of digital devices and the internet has made it easier for Indian art to be distributed to a global audience. Websites such as Instagram and Twitter allow Indian artists to use their artwork to communicate a wide range of ideas and topics. Public galleries and exhibitions have also been enabled by the internet, allowing Indian artists to promote and display their work to larger audiences.

Indian art in the digital age has seen immense growth and progress. Long gone are the days when Indian artwork was confined to paper and canvas; today, digital and online platforms have greatly expanded the range of tools and mediums which Indian artists can use to express their creativity. As these tools continue to evolve and advance, Indian artwork can only be expected to continue to evolve and innovate, giving the public glimpses into the talented and creative minds of contemporary Indian artist.

"Indian painting uses vibrant colors to create a unique
atmosphere that is both meditative and enlightening."
– Abanindranath Tagore

XIV

The ongoing relevance and significance of Indian Art & Painting

Indian Art and Painting have had a long and diverse history, dating back to the prehistoric era. Indian art and painting have been an important source of religious, social, cultural, and aesthetic expression throughout India's history. It has been used to illustrate religious doctrines and beliefs, to express a variety of aesthetic ideas, as well as to convey messages and ideas of political importance.

India's ancient art and painting often serve as visual reminders of great past events. A good example is the

Sanchi Stupa in Madhya Pradesh, which contains sculptures and carvings dating back to the Mauryan period (322-185 BCE). These carvings offer insights into the culture and society of the Mauryan era. In addition, the Ajanta and Ellora caves in Maharashtra are a treasure trove of Hindu and Buddhist art and painting, offering a glimpse into India's religious past.

In the modern age, Indian art and painting have continued to play an important role in Indian culture. Artists, such as Kapila Vatsyayan and M. F. Husain, have created new ways of expressing Indian themes and made Indian art more accessible to a wider audience. In addition, many Indians are now using art and painting to express their contemporary cultural, religious, and political views.

Indian Art and Painting have also gained global recognition. Many collectors, curators, and galleries in the West are now interested in India's art and painting, which is being showcased in various venues. This has led to increased exposure for Indian artists and greater opportunities for them to sell their works both in India and abroad.

Finally, Indian art and painting have served as a unifying force among Indians. Whether they are living in India or abroad, many Indians are joining art classes or organizations to learn about the history and evolution of Indian art and painting. In this way, Indian art and painting continue to bond Indians together across religious and cultural boundaries.

In conclusion, Indian art and painting have played an important role throughout India's history and continue to remain relevant in the contemporary era. It illustrates India's rich history and culture, and it has served as both a unifying force and an avenue of creativity. Indian art and painting is an integral part of India's identity, and it is an invaluable asset to the country and the world.

"Indian painting is an expression of the vibrant culture
and people of India." – Satyajit Ray

XV

Ancient Indian Art and Painting: Indus Valley Civilization and Vedic Period

Ancient Indian art and painting can be traced back to the Indus Valley Civilization and the Vedic Period. The Indus Valley Civilization, which flourished in the north-western part of the Indian subcontinent between 3300 and 1300 BCE, is known for its exquisite art, which includes figurines, seals, and paintings. One of the most famous pieces of art from this period is the Great Bath of Mohenjo-daro, which is thought to be a ritual bathing complex. Additionally, the Indus Valley Civilization produced beautiful carvings of animals, such as bulls, elephants, and monkeys, as well as pottery and terracotta figurines.

The Vedic Period, which began around 1500 BCE, was the

period in which the Vedic texts were composed. This period was also known for its art, particularly its temple paintings, which were often very intricate and detailed. These paintings typically had religious themes, which included figures of gods, goddesses, and other mythical creatures. Additionally, the Vedic Period saw the development of a distinct style of painting, known as Madhubani, which is still practiced today.

Overall, the art and painting produced during the Indus Valley Civilization and the Vedic Period represent an important part of India's artistic history. These pieces of art, from the Great Bath of Mohenjo-daro to the intricate temple paintings of the Vedic Period, capture the beauty and complexity of India's ancient civilization. Moreover, the art from this period is still highly valued and appreciated, and it continues to inspire art and culture today.

Other Books Of The Author

1. The Moments When I Met God
2. Kashiyile Theertha Pathangal
3. GURU GYAN VANI
4. Abhiprerak Gita
5. ASSI SE JAIN GHAT TAK
6. Hopelessness of Arjuna
7. The Soul and It's True Nature
8. Sense of Action (Karma)
9. Action through Wisdom
10. Action through Wisdom
11. THEORY AND PRACTICAL OF EVERY ACTION
12. LOGICAL UNDERSTANDING OF THE SUPREME
13. THE IMPERISHABLE SUPREME
14. Yatra Nishadraj se Hanuman Ghat Tak
15. Yatra Karnatak Ghat se Raja Ghat Tak
16. Yatra Pandey Ghat se Prayagraj Ghat Tak
17. Yatra Ranjendra Prasad Ghat se Dattatreya Ghat Tak
18. YaatraSindhiya Ghat se Gwaliar Ghat Tak
19. Yatra Mangala Gauri Ghat se Hanuman Gadhi Ghat Tak
20. Yatra Gaay Ghat Se Nishad Ghat Tak
21. MAA GANGA, GHATEN EVM UTSAV
22. Ganga Arti Dev Deepavali evam Any Utsav
23. Potentials of Digitalized India
24. VEDIC CONSCIOUSNESS
25. A Brief Introduction to Vedic Science
26. Kashi ke Barah Jyotirling
27. IMPACT OF MOTIVATION
28. Let's have a Milky Way Journey

CONTACT

DR. JAGADEESH PILLAI

PhD in Vedic Science

Four Times Guinness World Record Holder

Winner of Mahatma Gandhi Vishwa Shanti Puraskar and
Global Peace Ambassador

Gemology, Astro & Vastu Consultant - Spiritual Counselor

Consultant for designing World Record Ideas

Efficient Tarot Card Reader

9839093003

myrichindia@gmail.com

drjagadeeshpillai@facebook

drjagadeeshpillai@instagram

jagadeeshpillai@youtube

www. JAGADEESHPILLAI.com

|| LOKAHA SAMASTHAHA SUKHINO BHAVANTU ||

• 81 •